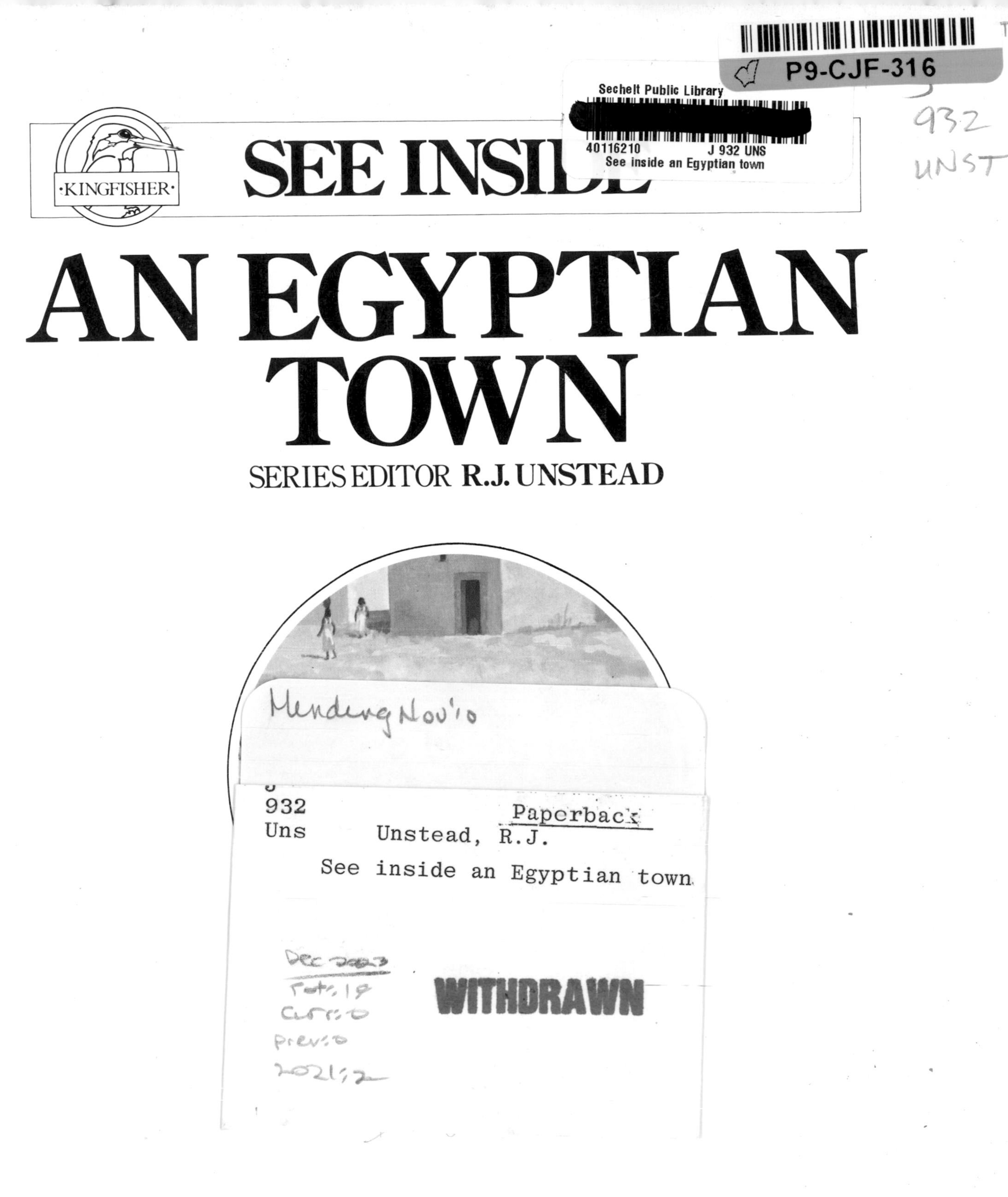

SEE INSIDE AN EGYPTIAN TOWN

SERIES EDITOR **R.J. UNSTEAD**

KINGFISHER BOOKS

CONTENTS

Series Editor and Author
R. J. Unstead

Illustrators
Bill Stallion, Linden Artists,
Francis Phillips, Roy Coombs

This revised edition published in 1986 by
Kingfisher Books Limited, Elsley Court,
20–22 Great Titchfield Street, London W1P 7AD
A Grisewood & Dempsey Company
Originally published in hardcover by
Hutchinson & Co (Publishers) Limited in 1977.

BRITISH LIBRARY CATALOGUING IN PUBLICATION DATA
Unstead, R. J.
See inside an Egyptian town.—2nd ed.—(See inside)
1. City and town life—Egypt—History—
Juvenile literature 2. Egypt—Social life and
customs—To 332 B.C.—Juvenile literature
3. Akhetaten (Ancient city)—Social life and customs
I. Title
932 DT61
ISBN 0-86272-206-3
Printed in Hong Kong

Below: Bust of Akhenaten, the strange young king who tried to replace worship of the old gods by a new religion, with a single universal god. In art, he encouraged a more realistic style; so, in statues and reliefs, he is seen to be a rather ugly man, with a big nose, thick lips and a fat belly. Left: A tomb painting of about 1400 BC from Thebes, the capital which Akhenaten abandoned.

Akhetaten

The city of Akhetaten stood on the east bank of the Nile about 325 km north of Thebes. Its building was begun in about 1375 BC at the orders of the ruling King who came to the throne as Amenhotep IV (also known as Amenophis IV).

For many years the greatest of the Egyptian gods had been Amun or Amen, once merely the local god of Thebes where his priests had become immensely rich and powerful. The young monarch Amenhotep came to believe that a god called Aten, 'the disk of the sun' was not merely greater than Amen and all the other Egyptian deities but was the only god.

He commanded his astonished people to worship only Aten and, in the fourth year of his reign, decided to replace Thebes, home of Amen, by a new capital, sacred to Aten. It must be built, he declared, in a place which 'belongs to no god, to no goddess, to no prince, to no princess' and, having found the site, he decreed that the capital be called Akhetaten, meaning 'Horizon of Aten'. His own name contained the hated name Amen, so he changed it to Akhenaten – 'It is well with the Aten'.

The site of the new city (known today as el-Amarna) was a D-shaped sandy plain about 9 kms long and 4½ kms wide at its widest point. The straight side of the D was the Nile from which the desert cliffs curved away.

By the king's orders, hundreds of workmen, architects, and officials must have been transported to the site by boat to lay out the town and erect its buildings, for, within two years it was advanced enough for Akhenaten to move there with his beautiful wife, Nefertiti, their little daughters, and all the nobles and court officials and servants. As far as we know, he never left it for a single day but, ignoring the rest of his kingdom, devoted the rest of his life to the growing capital.

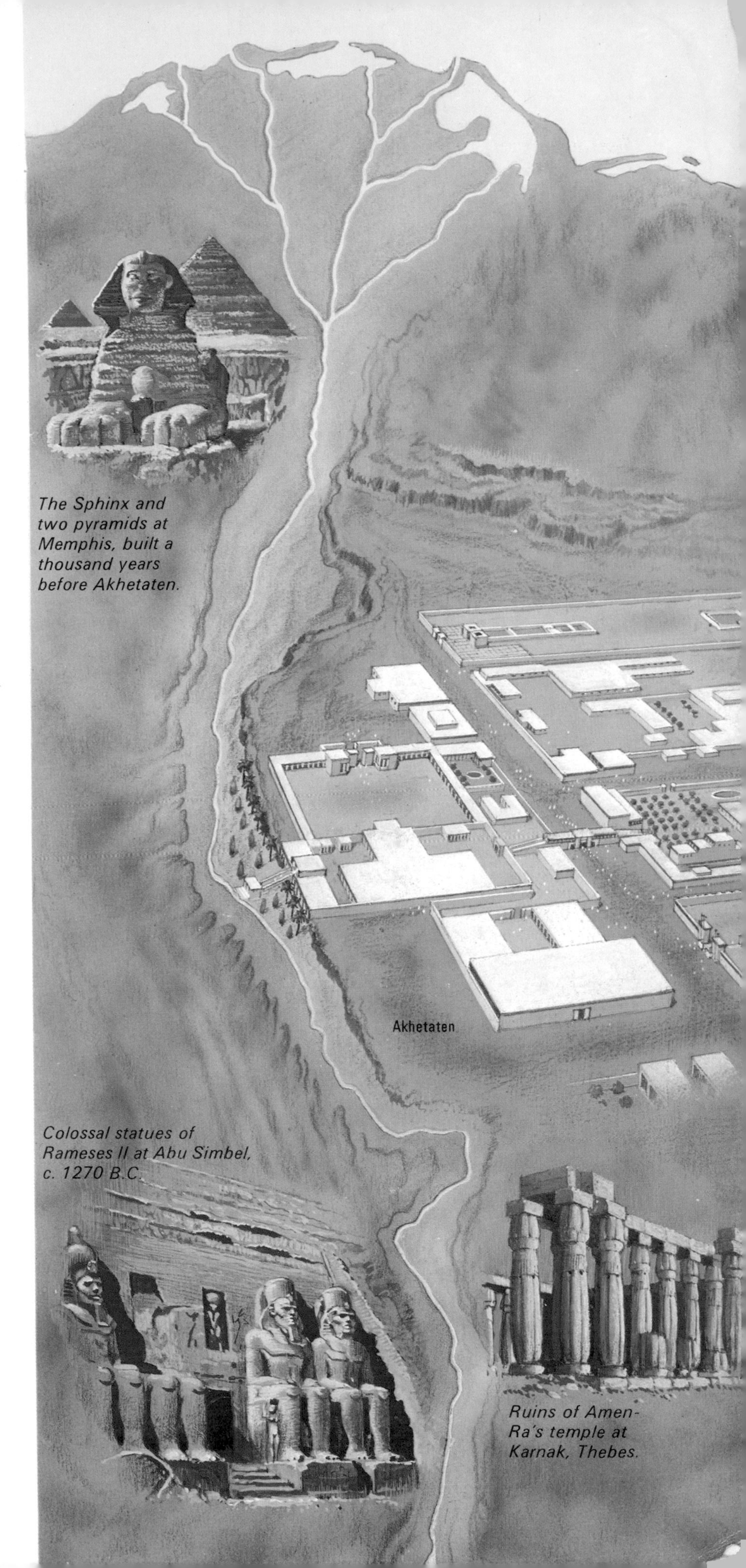

The Sphinx and two pyramids at Memphis, built a thousand years before Akhetaten.

Colossal statues of Rameses II at Abu Simbel, c. 1270 B.C.

Ruins of Amen-Ra's temple at Karnak, Thebes.

The Streets of Akhetaten

Akhetaten occupies a narrow strip several kilometres long and only one kilometre wide, because the fertile strip along by the river is too valuable to be built on, but it is useless to build out in the desert towards the cliffs because of the lack of water. So the city has had to be built along a strip of barren land where wells have been sunk to obtain water. There could be no question therefore of building a compact city surrounded by a wall. Instead, there are several areas of development spaced out along the strip – the Main City, with the Royal Palace and Temples, the North Suburb, South City and Palace of the Southern Pool (called Maru-Aten). There is also, strangely enough, a Workmen's Village, well inland on the desert and far from any water supply.

King's Way, the most westerly and important thoroughfare, connects Maru-Aten to the Main Centre and then runs on to the most northerly tip on the site. All the main roads are wide – as much as 50 metres in places – and without any paving whatsoever. Lesser streets connect the main roads, more or less at right angles, but there is nothing neat and regular about them. Some of them twist like lanes and occasionally open out into a little square with a well in the middle. Even the major roads are not continuously straight, for, in places, a road has to go round a house that for some reason has been built in its path.

Right: An artist's reconstruction of ancient Akhetaten, the new capital founded by the pharaoh Akhenaten. After his death the city was abandoned and the royal court returned to Thebes, the old capital. All the houses at Akhetaten were built at ground-floor level. This was doubtless because the town was built on an empty site.

THE NILE WATERWAY

The river front has been built along with quays and wharves for the unending arrival and departure of boats bringing foodstuffs, materials and merchandise of every kind, as well as traders, artists, craftsmen, provincial governors, foreign ambassadors and their attendants. Across the river, a huge area of land has been put under cultivation to provide food.

12
10
11
9
7
1
3
4
6
8
5

Building a House

In Akhetaten, houses are very much alike; that is, the house of one rich noble is similar to all the other houses belonging to rich nobles. The same is true of middle-class houses, and a workman's hovel is like all the other hovels.

Basically, a house consists of a main central room with smaller rooms grouped round it to keep it cool in summer and warm in winter. The main room is built higher than the other rooms, so that windows can be placed near ceiling level to let in light.

Houses of both rich and poor are made of sun-dried bricks, for the annual flooding of the Nile leaves behind vast quantities of mud, providing an unlimited supply of cheap building material. When the wet mud has been prepared, the brick-maker uses a hollow wooden mould to shape the brick, leaving it alongside rows of other bricks to dry in the hot sun. The size of bricks for housing measures about 23 × 11 × 8 cms, but larger ones, 33–37 × 15–16 × 9–10 cms are used for walls of palaces and temples.

In poor houses, the walls may be only one brick thick but,

Builders' tools, which include a set-square, mallet, plumb-line, dowel-peg and plasterer's smoothing trowel. They are made of wood and copper, for iron is almost unknown.

in most cases, builders lay a course at least two bricks thick, with a layer of mortar between each course. To finish off the outside, walls are given a coat of mud plaster that is sometimes white-washed but often left to dry in its natural colour. Mud plaster also serves to cover the floor, on top of a layer of bricks or, in poor houses, simply on the levelled ground.

Large tiles of mud are laid in some of the finer houses and painted in bright colours.

Wood is scarce and expensive, because Egypt's native trees, the palm, acacia and sycamore, cannot be sawn into planks or will provide only short lengths of timber. Palm trunks can be used for posts and sawn lengthways for ceiling beams, but all the other timber has to be imported, usually from Lebanon where cedar grows abundantly. Wood is therefore used sparingly; as a rule, only for columns, doors and staircase supports. The wooden columns supporting the roof stand on circular limestone bases and, in better houses, stone is used for thresholds, doorways and lintels, which are carved with the name and titles of the owner, if he is a man of importance.

These small houses, often built alongside mansions of the rich, have flat roofs with the usual light shelter providing shade. The staircase comes up from the entrance hall or kitchen. Notice the bread oven in the yard.

On the building site above, workmen are fetching water to be mixed with the mud by foot and hoe. Chopped straw is trodden in to improve the strength and binding quality. The brickmakers are said to 'strike' bricks when they lay them in rows to dry for two or three days. Labourers carry finished bricks to a half-built house on slings attached to a yoke balanced on one shoulder.

A Nobleman's Villa

On the King's Way, in North Suburb, stands a nobleman's residence which has become the best known house in Akhetaten, because enough of it has survived for over three thousand years to give an accurate picture of its layout and decoration. Basically it resembles nearly every other house in the town, for its main feature is a central living-room surrounded by lots of other rooms.

The house stands (or rather stood, for only ruins are left) in extensive grounds, surrounded by a high wall. You enter by a towered gateway (1) and, having been checked in by a gatekeeper, whose lodge is to your left (2), you walk up a tree-lined path to the family place of worship, a little temple (3) fronted by a flight of steps and a pair of painted columns. The path turns right to lead you into an inner courtyard from which you enter the house by a flight of shallow steps, passing through a doorway framed in stone, its lintel carved with the owner's name. From the porch you go through a vestibule (4) and are led by a servant into the North Loggia (5). This is a handsome reception room (loggia means a kind of verandah). From here you enter the Central Hall (6), the heart of the house, (see pages 10–11).

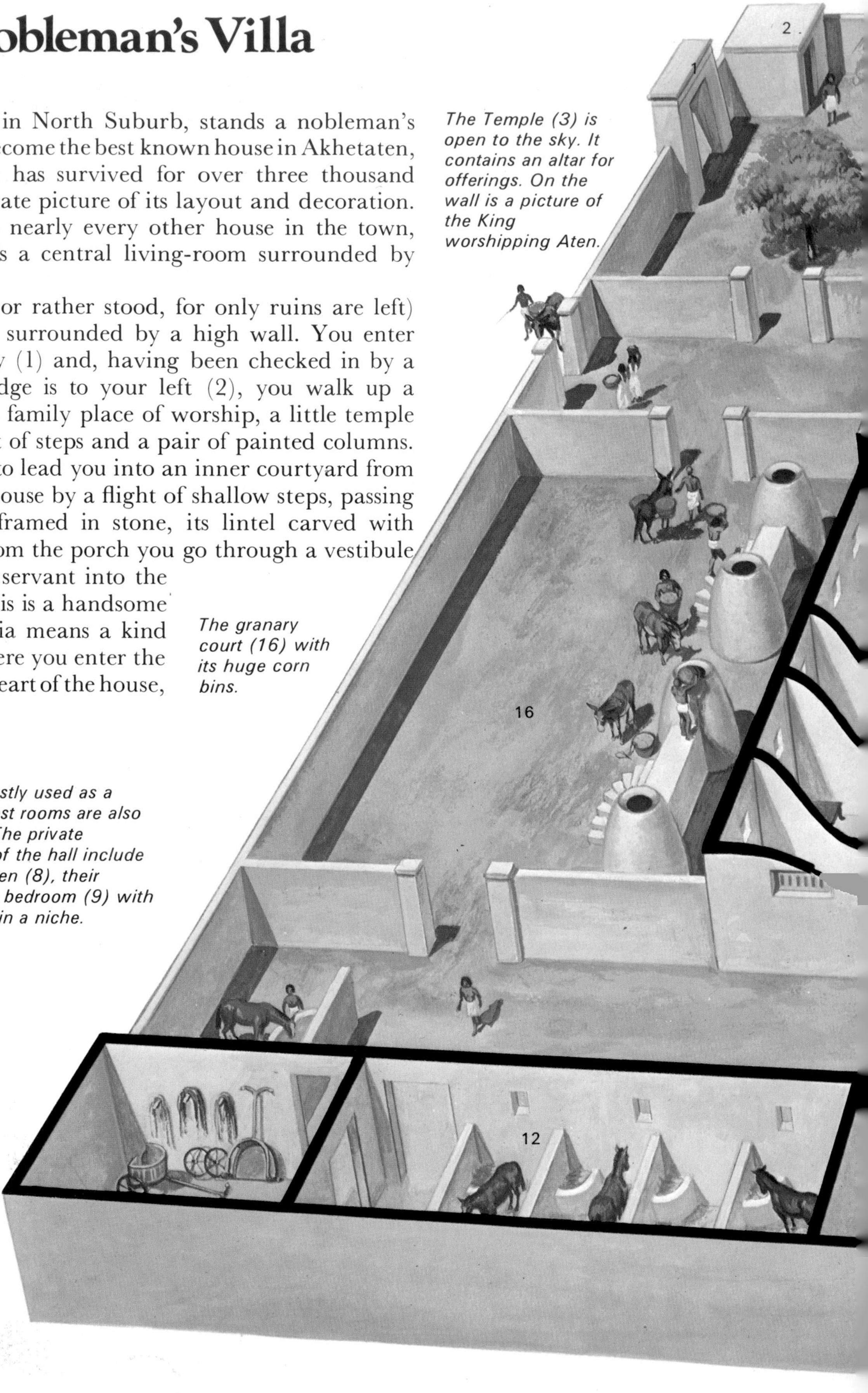

The Temple (3) is open to the sky. It contains an altar for offerings. On the wall is a picture of the King worshipping Aten.

The granary court (16) with its huge corn bins.

The West Loggia (7) is mostly used as a sitting-room in winter. Guest rooms are also on this side of the house. The private quarters on the other side of the hall include a sitting-room for the women (8), their bedrooms and the master's bedroom (9) with his bed standing on a dais in a niche.

The bathroom (10) contains a small slab on which the master lies while a slave pours water over him. Beyond the bathroom is the lavatory.

Stables (12), servants' quarters (13), kitchen (14) and cattle-yard (15) are on the southern and eastern sides, because the prevailing wind will carry away the smells.

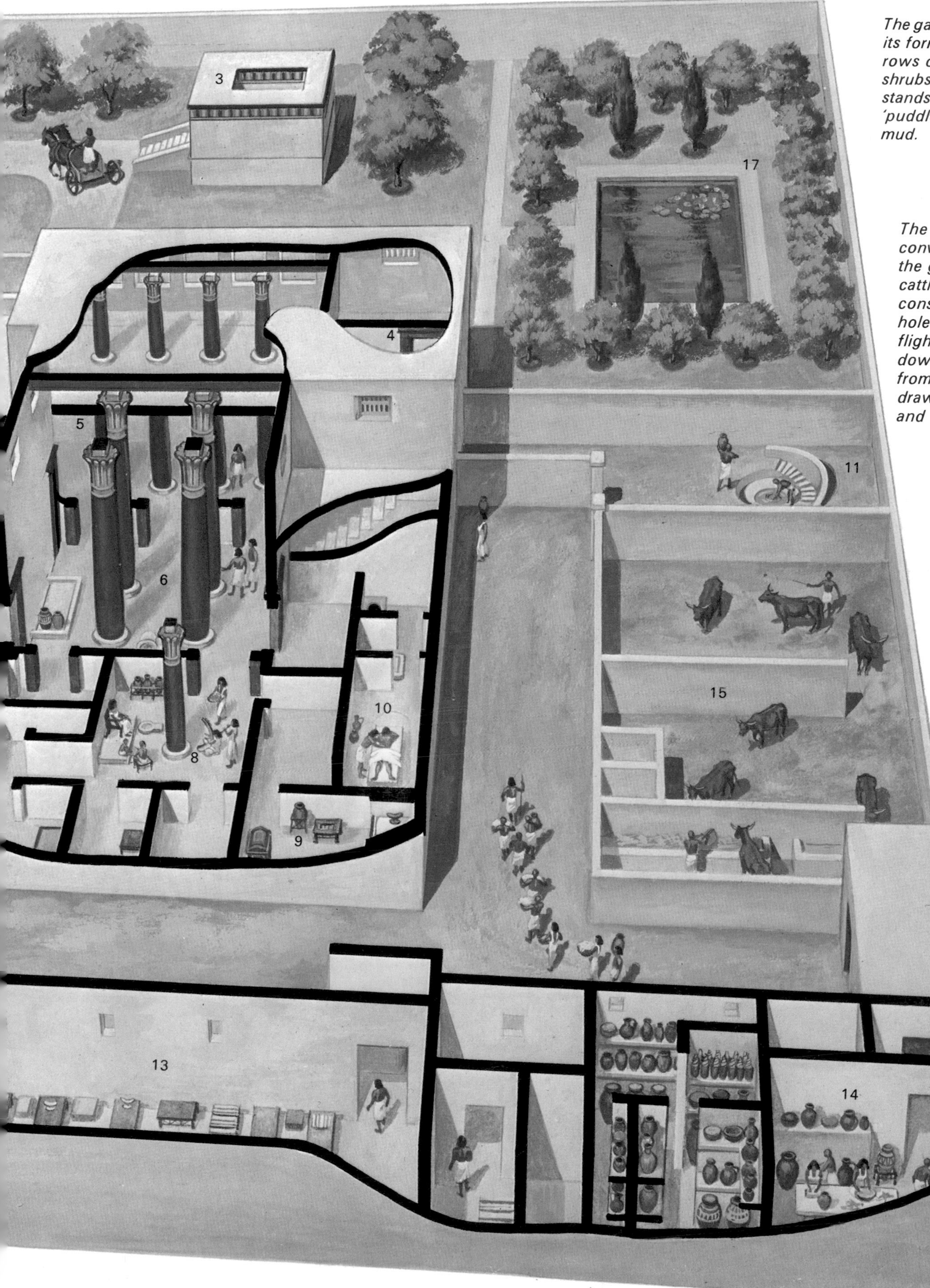

The garden (17) with its formal pool and rows of trees and shrubs. Every plant stands in its 'puddle' of river mud.

The well (11) conveniently near the garden and cattle-yard. It consists of a wide hole in which a flight of steps leads down to a platform from which water is drawn up by a rope and bucket.

The Central Hall

The Central Hall is the heart of a nobleman's residence. The lofty blue painted ceiling is supported by four pillars, and, high up, close to the ceiling, there are several small windows with vertical bars.

The room contains two interesting features. Against one wall is a low brick dais on which the master and his principal guests sit on mats and small stools made of wood and stone. Next to the dais is a brick hearth on which a brazier filled with burning charcoal is placed on cool evenings. On the other side of the room is the *lustration* slab, a limestone slab with a raised edge and a runnel to carry water off into a vase standing at the side. A servant pours water from another vase over the hands and feet of a visitor who has come in from the dusty city, and dries them with a linen towel.

Notice the number of recesses or niches in the walls, gaily painted in panels of red and yellow. They are there to satisfy the Egyptians' love of balance; if a door on one side of the room is not matched by another opposite, then a niche is put there instead. Similarly, if there are real windows at the top of three sides of the walls, identical windows are painted on the fourth side.

From the Central Hall a staircase leads up to the roof where a light shelter has been built to provide shade from the sun, and where you can get a fine view of the whole estate.

The walls of private houses are not covered with painted scenes as in the royal palaces, but are finished in soft colours. Columns are usually red and the cross-rafters pink, while the ceiling may be decorated with rosettes, with a frieze of fruit and flowers running along the upper part of the room.

A family scene in the Central Hall of a nobleman's house. The master and his wife are seated on the left with one of their children, while two guests play draughts with pieces like halma-men. Notice the pet cats, the elegant furniture, and wine jar.

TIME TO RELAX

The King's earnest preoccupation with religion does not deter his people from enjoying themselves. They are affectionate kindly people who love social life, music and dancing. A wealthy householder hires musicians, like the harpist in this picture, and professional dancers to entertain his guests at parties and banquets. Some people place a cone on their head made of scented pomade which melts in the warm atmosphere and drenches the hair with sweet-smelling ointment. It is customary for young children to go naked, while maidservants and slaves normally wear only a girdle or a loincloth.

The Great Temple

The greatest and most important building in the city is the Great Temple of Aten, the centre of worship of the new god. It stands in a huge rectangular enclosure or *timenos*, some 800 metres long and 300 metres wide, surrounded by a high boundary wall. Should you be granted the privilege of entering the Temple, you do so from the west end of the enclosure, passing between tall pylon towers into a courtyard where you see ahead of you the massive

Set in the north wall, below, is a large building called the Hall of Foreign Tribute, in which flights of steps ascend to the King's throne, set on a platform beneath a richly decorated canopy. Here Akhenaten and Nefertiti receive gifts and taxes from visiting princes and ambassadors. Inside the walls of the enclosure is a huge slaughter yard where cattle are killed and the carcasses prepared for the offering tables.

A remarkable feature of the Temple is the presence on either side of the causeway of rows and rows of squat mud-brick pillars about one metre high. These are offering tables which are piled with fruit, flowers, vegetables and meat. Incense vases stand between them and the chapels. Outside the walls of Per-Hai and Gem-Aten are more of these offering tables, no fewer than 900 on each side. They are for the use of ordinary persons not privileged to enter the Temple.

Sanctuary

Slaughter Yard

Akhenaten and Queen Nefertiti accompanied by a little princess, make offerings of fruit and flowers to Aten, in the Sanctuary of the Great Temple.

front of Per-Hai, the House of Rejoicing. In front of its stone-faced towers stand ten immense flagpoles with fluttering pennants and you pass through a hall filled with columns and adorned with wall-carvings of the King and Queen.

From Per-Hai, you reach the next part of the Temple, Gem-Aten – the Finding of Aten. Ahead of you stretches a long, narrow court, with an altar approached by a flight of steps, and beyond the altar, a causeway that runs towards another pair of lofty columns. This brings you into a second court, then into a third and finally into three smaller sanctuary courts, one leading into another, and each with its central altar and surrounding chapels. There is no exit from the eastern end of Gem-Aten, nor from the sides, so the King, Queen and priests have to return to the entrance after they have worshipped at the High Altar of the farthest, most secluded court.

At the eastern end of the Temple enclosure stands the Sanctuary, where, again, we enter a walled court and pass between pylons into a second court dominated by huge columns and four colossal statues of King Akhenaten. Screen walls block the view ahead, but a passage leads into the heart of the Sanctuary, the Holy of Holies, with the High Altar and surrounding chapels all open to the sky.

When you enter a traditional Egyptian temple to a god such as Amen, Ptah or Horus, you go from the sunshine into a gloomy colonnade, then into a dim hall and, as the floor rises and the roof lowers, into the darkness of the Sanctuary. In this awesome atmosphere, priests wash, anoint, clothe, feed and worship the god's statue every day. The Temple of Aten is quite different, for he is the god of sunshine and light, so the courts are open to the sky and worship takes place to the accompaniment of music and singing.

The Fruits of the Nile

The peasants who work the royal lands on the west bank live over there in villages of small huts and probably never visit the new city on the other side of the Nile.

The *Cultivation* is the name given to the fairly narrow strip of land on both sides of the Nile on which it is possible to grow crops because the soil can be watered by the annual flooding and by irrigation canals.

At Akhetaten, the cultivatable land on the east (or city) bank is used mainly for ornamental pleasure gardens. Farming, to produce food for the city population and offerings for the temple, takes place on the west bank.

Here, you can see a busy scene at harvest-time: workers are cutting the grain near the top of the stems, while others load the ripe ears into baskets which are carried to the threshing-floor. Cattle are treading out the grain, as men fork away the spent ears. Nearby, the mixed grain and chaff are tossed into the air with wooden winnowing fans so that the wind carries the chaff away. The clean grain is placed in baskets whose numbers are noted down by a scribe.

In the picture, there are also gardens in which general crops are grown, some beehive-shaped granaries and a herd of goats. Boats, laden with produce, are crossing the river to the city wharves. The farming year begins in November, when the *inundation* or annual flooding has ended. The damp rich earth is ploughed by teams of oxen and then sown by sowers who sometimes walk ahead of the plough and sometimes behind it, and the seed is trodden into the ground by sheep and goats. Harvesting takes place in spring and finishes by May. Principal crops are *emmer* (a kind of wheat) and barley used mostly for making beer, the chief drink of the Egyptians. Flax is grown for making linen which everyone needs, since it is almost the only material used for clothes.

Gardens, which have to be watered regularly from ditches and pools, produce fruit and vegetables, such as beans, lettuce, lentils, onions, leeks, melons, gourds, figs, and pomegranates.

OFFERINGS FOR ATEN

Much care is taken in growing masses of flowers for the temple of Aten. Animals and birds are reared not only for food but also for religious sacrifices. Oxen and sheep are more valuable than pigs and goats, while donkeys are the beasts of burden. The finest cattle are raised in the Delta, but there is enough grazing for small herds near the villages of Upper Egypt. Geese are kept for the table and for sacrifice, as well as ducks and pigeons.

The Pharaoh's Pleasure Garden

The Great Palace in the main city is not the king's only residence. About two kilometres south of the city stands Maru-Aten, the Palace of the Southern Pool. It consists of two oblong enclosures, the smaller one containing a handsome pavilion with a great columned hall and a throne room. In the grounds is a small lake surrounded by trees. A gate leads through the wall into a larger enclosure almost filled by a shallow lake. A stone pier runs out into the water with steps at the end from which guests can go aboard the pleasure boats. In the garden stands another pavilion where the king may choose to rest and perhaps entertain his courtiers, for it contains two wine cellars. There is also a chapel and a water garden or aquarium with tanks for fish or water plants. Behind a screen wall stand the little houses of workmen who look after this estate, and the kennels of the royal greyhounds.

A kilometre or so north of the Temple stands the Northern Palace which has been built to cater for the king's love of nature, for it contains a zoological garden, with enclosures for cattle and antelope, an artificial lake and aviaries where Akhenaten spends hours watching the rare and beautiful birds.

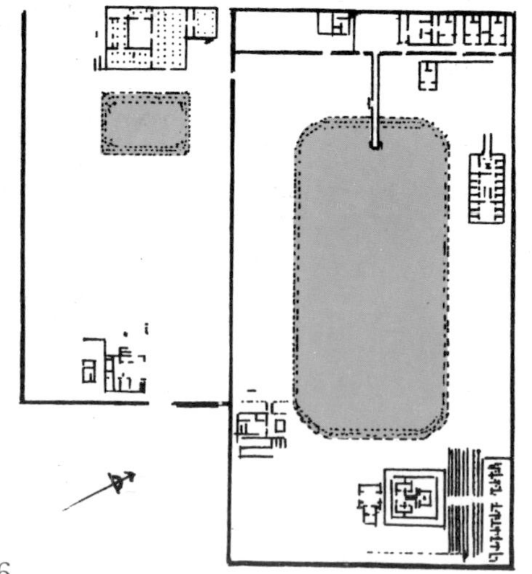

Plan of the enclosures at Maru-Aten.

Servants set the table with fruit, flowers and wine for the royal picnic.

Queen Nerfertiti, Akhenaten's beautiful wife, with their three little daughters.

King Akhenaten in a pensive mood. He is a poet who composes hymns to Aten, the sun god.

A girl harpist and a fan-bearer, a slave from Nubia, a part of the Empire lying south of Egypt.

The Workmen's Village

In the desert to the east of the city is a hollow in which lies a walled village. This is a curious spot for any kind of habitation, since it is far from the river and from any well or canal, so that every drop of water, as well as all stores, have to be transported by donkey.

The village itself is equally strange, for it consists of 73 small houses, all exactly the same size and of almost identical layout. There is one larger house belonging to the overseer. The houses are built in terraces separated by five narrow streets, and the whole prison-like compound is surrounded by a strong wall in which there is only one gate.

It is clear that the villagers *are* prisoners, for guards patrol the roads running along the surrounding hills, and the wall seems intended, not to keep an enemy out, but to keep the inhabitants in. They are, in fact, tomb-workers, brought here to excavate and decorate the tombs in the nearby cliffs – work which fills ordinary citizens with dread, so that it is carried out by slaves, criminals and violent characters who are best confined to this walled enclosure far from the civilized life of Aten's city.

Some of the villagers have built a manger against the house wall for a cow or donkey.

Each cottage, five metres wide where it fronts on to the street and ten metres deep, contains four rooms – an entrance hall, living-room, bedroom, and kitchen. A staircase (usually in the hall) leads up to the roof on which there is generally a shelter made of matting and poles, though here and there a householder has built a little room with mud-brick walls. The entrance hall has a window close under the roof and the living-room, built higher than the other rooms, has windows looking over the flat roof.

The villagers make no attempt to decorate the outside of their mud-brick houses, but indoors, the rooms are usually white-washed or decorated with frescoes of flower patterns and even human figures, painted with materials the workmen bring home from the tomb chapels.

The entrance hall (1) contains the workman's tools, the weaving loom and often a manger for the family goat.

The living-room (2) contains a low brick dais covered with mats and cushions, the great round-bottomed water-jar and stools. There is a hearth for a charcoal fire and, at night, the room is lit by lamps consisting of saucers with a flickering wick floating in oil.

The kitchen (3) is furnished with a brick bread oven, shaped like a big pot, bins and baskets for grain and other food, a mortar and pestle for grinding wheat and sundry bowls and cooking pots.

3
2
1
Stallion

Rock Tombs

In the rocky cliffs which lie east of the city, the King has presented his leading officials with sites for their tombs, which have been excavated by gangs from the Workmen's Village. Aten may have taken the place of all the other gods, but Egyptians still believe in a life after death and in the importance of a tomb which preserves a dead man's body, with scenes showing how he has served the king in this life.

Quarriers cut into the cliff to make a corridor, which becomes T-shaped when a cross corridor is cut at the farther end. A burial chamber (1) contains a deep shaft-grave and, beyond the cross corridor, lies the shrine with a statue of the dead man (2). The roof is upheld by columns shaped and decorated to resemble papyrus stalks and the tomb walls are smoothed so that they can be covered with pictures and scenes created by the sculptors and painters.

All the tombs contain sculptures glorifying the King whom we see, usually accompanied by the Queen, making offerings to Aten or arriving in his chariot at the Temple or rewarding his loyal servants with gold necklaces which he places about their necks. We also see details of everyday life – single-masted cargo ships, for instance, at their river moorings, a fort with a guard on duty, peasants with cattle and donkeys, running messengers, and criminals caught by the police and being handed over to the city officials.

Work is going on at several tombs at the same time. They belong to such important people as Huya, the Royal Chamberlain, Penthu, the King's Physician, Nay, Bearer of the Fan, Panehsy, Chief Priest of Aten, and Mahu, Chief of Police.

Between the Workmen's Village and the cliffs are some tomb chapels (below) built of mud brick and each containing a brilliantly decorated shrine in which offerings of food and drink will be placed for the middle-class owner who is to be buried in one of the shaft graves a little distance away.

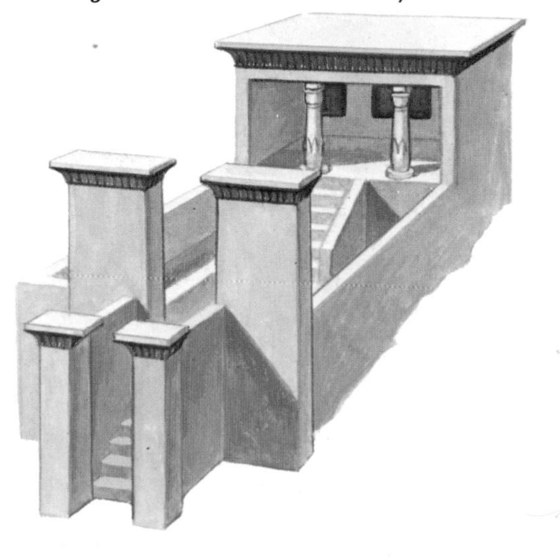

A ROYAL TOMB

The king and his family are to be buried in the Royal Tomb which is being built about 6 kms away in a *wadi* or dried up water course that cuts through the cliffs. Here, a great many tomb chambers are being excavated and decorated with reliefs showing scenes of worship. None is finished yet, apart from the tomb of the little Princess Maketaten who died young.

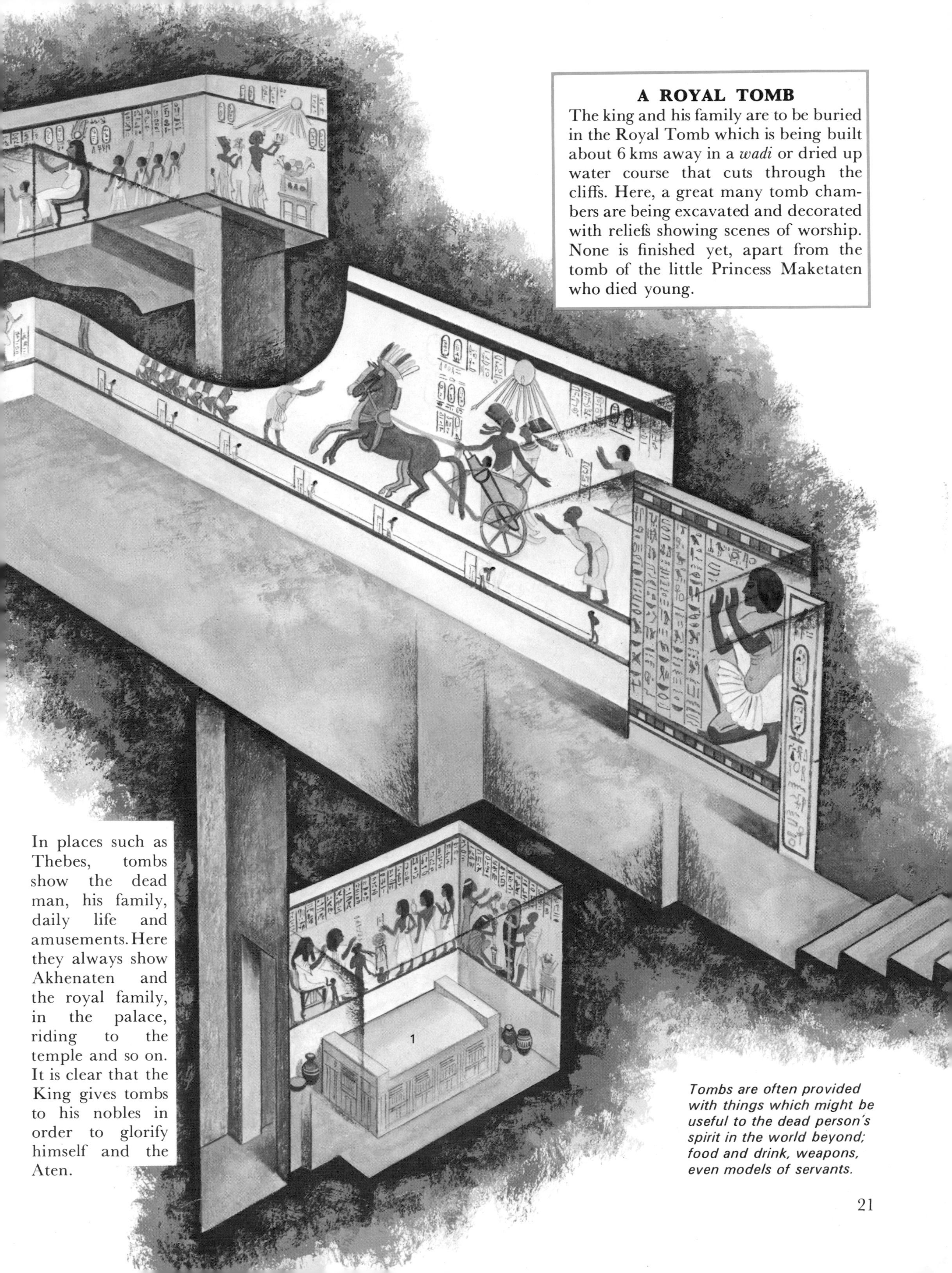

In places such as Thebes, tombs show the dead man, his family, daily life and amusements. Here they always show Akhenaten and the royal family, in the palace, riding to the temple and so on. It is clear that the King gives tombs to his nobles in order to glorify himself and the Aten.

Tombs are often provided with things which might be useful to the dead person's spirit in the world beyond; food and drink, weapons, even models of servants.

The End of the Story

The death mask made of beaten gold inlaid with semi-precious stones which covered the face of Tutankhamen's mummy. It is of the finest workmanship and is a realistic portrait of the young king.

Tutankhamen the harpooner stands on a raft ready to throw his harpoon.

Akhenaten's dream city was inhabited for only a few years. Built at tremendous speed, it was abandoned even more quickly after the 'heretic' King's death.

Things had been going wrong for some time before that, for Akhenaten's mother, Queen Ty, had made a state visit to the city to warn her son that in giving all his heart and mind to the new religion, he was neglecting his kingdom. Outlying provinces were under attack from the Hittites; allies begged in vain for help and, at home, the cost of the new capital and the King's neglect of his duties were causing unrest.

Perhaps Akhenaten decided to take some action; perhaps Queen Nefertiti, devoted to the new religion, opposed him. We cannot be sure, but it seems that a terrible quarrel resulted in Nefertiti's disgrace and retirement to a palace in the north end of the city, probably with the young prince Tutankhaten. Two years later, Akhenaten died and Tutankhaten, aged nine, was proclaimed king. Probably because of his mother's influence, he was not made to return to Thebes immediately, but when she died in about the third year of the reign, the priests of Amen had their way. The king changed his name to Tutankhamen and was received in Thebes with great honour and rejoicing. Not long afterwards he died and was buried amid fabulous riches.

Akhetaten had been partially abandoned. The nobles and Court officials shut up their fine houses but doubtless many people stayed on. However a few years later, a king named Horemheb decided to wipe out every trace of the heretic city. Temples, palaces and mansions were razed to the ground, the tombs were desecrated and the name of Akhenaten hacked out wherever it occurred. For centuries, the city's very existence was forgotten until, in 1887, a peasant woman unearthed some clay tablets which proved to be diplomatic letters sent to Akhenaten's court. Excavation of the site began in 1891 and, although it has never been completed, enough has been discovered to enable us to picture the city that flourished so briefly 3000 years ago.

Gods and Goddesses of Ancient Egypt

There were hundreds of gods, many of them local deities, from which some emerged as national gods. Many were shown with human bodies and animal or other shaped heads. Here are a few of them:

Amen
Also Amun, the great god of Thebes.

Anubis
The jackal-headed god of the dead and of embalmers. He performed the 'weighing of the heart' when the soul of a dead man was judged.

Aten
God of the sun-disk. The single god whose worship Akhenaten tried to establish in place of the other gods.

Bast
Cat-goddess of the Delta.

Bes
The dwarf with a lion's face, god of music, jollity and the home.

Geb
God of the earth, husband of Nut.

Hapy
The Nile god, shown as a man with heavy breasts.

Hathor
Cow-headed mother goddess of happiness, music, dancing and love. She was the wife of Horus.

Horus
The falcon-headed sky-god, son of Osiris and Isis, avenger of his father. The king became Horus during his life on earth.

Isis
Mother goddess, wife of Osiris and mother of Horus.

Khnum
The ram-headed god who made man on a potter's wheel.

Khons
The Moon god.

Maat
Goddess of truth, bearing an ostrich feather on her head.

Min
God of fertility.

Mut
Wife of Amen.

Nut
The sky-goddess whose curved body formed the arch of heaven.

Osiris
The god of death, rebirth and the Inundation. The story of how he was murdered and restored to life symbolized the rebirth of the harvests and of man.

Ptah
Principal god of Memphis, patron of craftsmen.

Re
Sun god of Heliopolis. Although the Egyptians had many other sun gods, Re or Ra was the name generally used.

Seth
God of violence, murderer of his brother, Osiris.

Thoeris
Hippopotamus goddess, patron of women in childbirth.

Thoth
Ibis-headed god of writing; scribe of the gods.

Overleaf: Part of a fresco painted on a wall of the tomb of Nebamun, chief sculptor at Thebes during the reign of Amenophis III. The goldsmiths and joiners are skilled craftsmen who made precious objects for tombs, temple offerings and the palaces of kings. The treasures found in the tomb of Tutankhamen are examples of their skill.

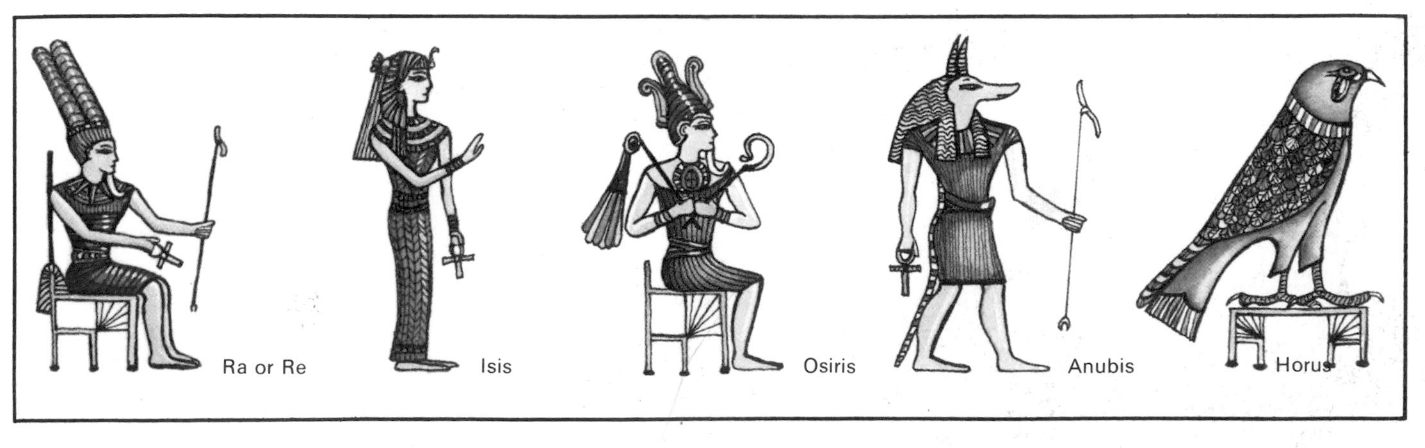

IMPORTANT HAPPENINGS

BC 3100 — **BC 1567** — **BC 30**

Note: Historians do not always agree on dates of events in Ancient Egypt. The spelling and form of some names vary; e.g. Amenhotep–Amenophis; Amen–Amun; Thotmes–Tuthmosis.

Egypt

***c*3100** First Egyptian Dynasty. Union of Upper and Lower Egypt by Menes, capital at Memphis. Copper tools, large-scale irrigation.
***c*2686–2181** The Old Kingdom. Pyramid Age: great pyramids and Sphinx built. Rise of Heliopolis and Re, the sun-god. Principal kings—Zoser, Cheops, Khafre and Pepi II. Wars with Libyans and Nubians. Timber imported, copper mined, stone used for building and sculpture. Rise of feudal nobles leads to decay of royal power.
2650 Death of Zoser for whom the first pyramid was built.
***c*2181–2050** First Intermediate Period. Disorder; break-up of united kingdom; pyramids robbed.
***c*2050–1786** The Middle Kingdom. Egypt re-united under Mentuhotep II. Thebes the capital; rise of the god Amen. Colossal temples and statues built. Nobles suppressed; Nubia conquered. Increase in wealth, culture.
***c*1786–1567** Second Intermediate Period. Invasion of Hyksos from Asia. Nubia and Lower Sudan regain freedom. Introduction of horse-chariots, bronze, improved weaving.
***c*1567–1085** The New Kingdom. XVIII Dynasty Pharaoh Ahmose I ousts the Hyksos. Under Amenhotep II, the Empire is enlarged from Nubia to the Euphrates, Queen Hatshepsut fosters trade, peace, building.
1420–1385 Golden Age of Egypt. Egypt reaches its zenith of power and wealth. Vast temples built at Luxor. Royal tombs in the Valley of the Kings. Amenhotep IV (Akhenaten) fails to establish Aten as sole god. Tutankhamen restores power of Amen-Re and Thebes. Horemheb destroys the city of Akhetaten.
1320–1200 XIX Dynasty. Seti I and Rameses II maintain the Empire, fight the Hittites. Great temples built at Abydos, Karnak and Abu Simbel
1200–1085 XX Dynasty. Rameses III, last of the great Pharaohs, repells the Libyans and Peoples of the Sea. Thereafter, military power declines, Asiatic provinces are lost, royal tombs are looted, and Egypt becomes lawless and poor.
1085–333 Late Dynastic Period. Egypt again divided: Libyan and, later, Nubian pharaohs occupy the throne.
***c*670** Assyrians sack Memphis and Thebes. A period of recovery follows with much trade in the Mediterranean.
525 Persians conquer Egypt but are later expelled, so that the XXX Dynasty is the last native house to rule.
343 Persians reconquer Egypt but are defeated by Alexander the Great upon his invasion of Egypt (332). After his death one of his generals founds the Ptolemaic Dynasty.
37 Mark Antony marries Cleopatra VII.
30 Romans under Octavian defeat Cleopatra and Mark Antony. Egypt becomes a Roman province.

Europe

***c*3000** New Stone Age in northern Europe.
***c*3000–1500** The Minoans flourish on the island of Crete.
***c*2000–1700** Greek-speaking tribes enter Greece.
***c*1800–1400** Stonehenge built in Britain (2nd–3rd phase).
***c*1600–1200** Mycenaean civilization flourishes in Greece.
***c*1500–1300** Bronze Age in northern Europe.
***c*1500** Volcanoes on the island of Thera erupt creating huge waves which engulf Crete.
***c*1450** Cretan civilization destroyed.
***c*1200** The end of the siege of Troy. After ten years, the Greeks led by Agamemnon capture Troy by hiding in the famous wooden horse.
***c*1200–800** Invaders from the north (especially by Dorians in the second half of the 12th century) start the collapse of the Mycenaean civilization. The Mycenaean kings speed it up by fighting among themselves.
***c*1100** Phoenician colonies in Spain.
***c*900** Rise of the Etruscans in Italy.
850–650 Rise of Greek city states.
776 Traditional date of the first Olympic Games. Apollo worshipped at Delphi.
753 Legendary date of Rome's founding.
***c*700** Halstatt culture—first use of iron.
600 Greeks found city of Massilia (now Marseilles) in France.
510 Founding of Roman Republic—Roman nobles drive out their Etruscan kings.
508 Athenian democracy begins.
494 Plebeians (common people) of Rome rebel against nobles. They win some rights.
460–429 Golden Age of Athens—Greek navy dominates the Aegean.
***c*450** Celtic La Tène culture develops in central and northern Europe.
431–404 Peloponnesian War between Athens and Sparta. Athens surrenders to Spartans.
380 Celts attack Rome.
336 Alexander of Macedon becomes King of the Greeks.
323 Alexander the Great dies aged 32.
215–168 Romans involved in wars in Greece.
55–54 Julius Caesar's expeditions to Britain.
44 Murder of Julius Caesar.
36–30 Struggles for rule of Rome between Mark Antony and Octavian.

Near East	East Asia	
***c*3100** First writing in Mesopotamia.		BC 3100
***c*2600–2400** Royal Graves of Ur. ***c*2372–2255** Akkadian Empire founded by Sargon in Sumeria. ***c*1800–1750** Hammurabi rules Babylon.	***c*2500** Indus Valley civilization arises in India. ***c*2000–1500** Legendary Hsia Dynasty in China.	
***c*1450–1180** Hittite Empire at its height. ***c*1200** Sea Peoples raid Mediterranean coasts. ***c*1150** Greeks begin to colonize coast of Asia Minor.	***c*1500** Indus Valley civilization falls to invaders. ***c*1500–1027** Shang Dynasty in China; the Bronze Age.	BC 1567
***c*973** Solomon becomes King of Israel. **705–682** Sennacherib becomes King of Assyria and establishes his capital at Nineveh (701). **670** Assyrians invade Egypt. **612** Medes and allies overthrow Assyrian Empire. **605–562** Nebuchadnezzar II rules as King of Babylon. **586** Nebuchadnezzar besieges Jerusalem. **539** Cyrus of Persia conquers Babylonia. **486–465** King Xerxes rules the Persian Empire. **360s** Revolts in Persian Empire. **334–330** Alexander the Great defeats the Persians in Asia Minor and Syria, takes Jerusalem, founds Alexandria in Egypt and, with the capture of Babylon, destroys the Persian Empire completely. **65–63** Romans conquer Syria and Palestine.	**1027–221** Western Chou Dynasty in China. **722–256** Eastern Chou Dynasty: Golden Age of Chinese philosophy, 'Warring States' period. **660** Jimmu Tenno, legendary first emperor of Japan accedes. **640** Birth of Chinese philosopher Lao-Tzu. ***c*600** Early cities around river Ganges, India. **563** The Buddha born in Nepal, India. **551** Birth of Chinese philosopher Confucius. **533** Persians invade India, by now highly civilized, with towns, cities and extensive overseas trade. North-west India becomes a province of Persian Empire for 200 years. Introduction of Persian art and religion. **327** Alexander the Great invades north India. **305** Chandragupta drives Greeks from India; founds Mauryan Empire. **274–232** Emperor Ashoka reigns in India. Buddhism becomes widespread. **221–206** Ch'in Dynasty in China; Great Wall completed. Huang Ti imposes military rule. **206** Western Han Dynasty begins in China (lasts until AD 8). Period of great achievement. ***c*185–AD 320** Invaders (Asiatic Greeks, Scythians, Parthians and Kushans) settle in north India and Punjab. **140–87** Han Emperor Wu Ti conquers Manchuria, Korea, southern China, makes contact with Vietnam, India and Rome. **52** The Huns become subject to the Chinese emperor.	BC 30

GLOSSARY OF TERMS

Archaic Period The time between the Unification and the Old Kingdom—the I and II Dynasties.

Amulets Small charms worn as jewellery in life and also placed in mummy wrappings to ward off evil spirits.

Amulets were thought to have magical powers.

Ankh The cross-like symbol of life, often carried by gods.

Book of the Dead A papyrus scroll of instructions and prayers, placed in a tomb to assist the dead man on his perilous journey to the after-life.

Canopic jars Four jars in which the internal organs of the body were preserved to protect them for the after-life. The lids were shaped like animal heads that were symbols of the four sons of Horus, who were the special guardians of these parts of the body.

Cartouche An oval shape, containing the King's name in hieroglyphs.

Clerestory Windows set between the top of walls and the roof to let light into central halls.

Colossus A huge statue of a god or king.

Demotic A kind of writing, more advanced than hieroglyphs, used for everyday business. It was developed around 700 BC.

Dynasty A succession of rulers of the same family making a division or period of Egyptian history. For example, the Ptolemaic Dynasty were the descendants of the ruler Ptolemy.

Embalming The process of preserving a body by soaking it in oils and spices. Beforehand, all the body's liquids have to be dried out.

Heretic Somebody who believes in a different idea or religion from the one most commonly accepted.

Hieratic A development of hieroglyphic writing in which scribes used signs rather than pictures.

Hieroglyphic The written language of the Egyptians. It consisted of picture symbols, sometimes representing words, sometimes consonants.

Hyksos People of uncertain origin who migrated, probably from Palestine, into Egypt over a long period. By *c*1680 BC, they gained control of northern Egypt, which they ruled for about 120 years, until driven out by Ahmose or Amosis I, founder of the XVIII Dynasty.

Hypostyle Hall of a temple whose roof was supported by many columns.

Inundation Every year in June, heavy rainfall in the Ethiopian mountains caused the Nile to rise and overflow its banks until most of Egypt was a vast lake. In September, the waters began to subside, leaving behind a layer of fertile silt which had only to be ploughed and sown with seed to produce the wonderful crops which were the basis of Egypt's wealth.

Ka The spirit of a man which lived on after death and for whom offerings of food and drink were placed in the tomb.

Kiosk Shelter on the roof of a house.

Kohl The eye-paint used by the ancient Egyptians and some Near Eastern people today. It was usually black or green. It was made from various stones ground into powder and then mixed with water. Kohl was worn by both sexes.

Late Period The XXVI to the XXXI Dynasties. The time when Egypt was conquered by the Assyrians and Persians, but had some periods of independence.

Lower Egypt The northern region of the country. It was a separate kingdom before 3118 BC when it was united with Upper Egypt by King Menes.

Lute A musical instrument, played by plucking strings with a pick.

The mummy of a priestess lies inside this painted coffin.

Mastaba The private tomb of a noble of the Old Kingdom. It consisted of two parts—burial chamber below ground and chapel, decorated with scenes from daily life.

Memphis The capital of the Old Kingdom, situated on the west bank of the Nile, not far from the pyramids and modern Cairo.

Middle Kingdom The XI, XII and XIII Dynasties, from *c*2060 to 1633 BC; a period of strong government and great achievements.

Mummy A body (from which internal organs were removed) treated with natron and ointments and wrapped in bandages to preserve it from decay.

Natron A sodium compound used mainly in mummification, but also in cooking and making glass and medicine.

New Kingdom The third great period, covering the XVIII to the XX Dynasties (*c*1567–1085 BC) when ancient Egypt reached its peak as a military power.

Nubia A large tract of country lying south of Upper Egypt, Nubia possessed rich reserves of gold, iron-ore and timber. It was also known as the Kingdom of Kush.

Obelisk An upright granite pillar with pointed gilded tip. Obelisks were connected with worship of Ra, the sun god, especially in early times at Heliopolis and later at Thebes.

Old Kingdom The III to the VI Dynasties (*c*2700–2140 BC), the Pyramid Age, when Egypt was united under Kings ruling from Memphis.

Ostracon A fragment of pottery or stone. Letters, bills, poems, children's lessons and sums were written on ostraca.

Papyrus A tall reed with a feathery head, used for making paper, light boats, rope, baskets and sandals. The word can also mean a document written on papyrus.

Pharaoh Meaning royal palace, the word came to be applied to the King. The Pharaoh was also regarded as a god.

Pre-dynastic period The period before the Unification of Egypt.

Pshent The double crown of Upper and Lower Egypt. The White Crown of Upper Egypt was high and conical. The Red Crown of Lower Egypt had a curious high back. Together they showed the unity of both parts of the Kingdom.

Ptolemaic Period The 300-year rule by the descendants of Ptolemy, who was a general of Alexander the Great. The dynasty ended with Cleopatra VII, who committed suicide when the Romans invaded Egypt in 30 BC.

Punt, the land of The land somewhere by the Red Sea, with which the Egyptians traded to buy incense and myrrh trees.

Pylons The great twin towers at the entrance to a temple.

Rosetta Stone A stela or stone slab discovered by Napoleon's soldiers at Rosetta, near Alexandria. The inscription was written in hieroglyphs, Demotic and Greek, which enabled Jean-François Champollion to decipher Egyptian hieroglyphs.

Sarcophagus Casing for a coffin made of wood, stone or gold.

Scribe An official who wrote things down and kept records of public events, temple construction, irrigation works, crops, wages and so on.

Shaduf A simple but invaluable irrigation machine, consisting of a long pole attached to an upright post. At one end of the pole was a counterweight, at the other end a rope with a bucket which could be lowered into the river and easily brought up and emptied into a ditch or furrow.

Sphinx A mythical beast with the head of a man and the body of a lion. The most famous is the Great Sphinx at Giza. It has the head of King Khafre.

Thebes Capital of the New Kingdom, on the east bank of the Nile, Thebes became a magnificent city. It was the centre of worship for the sun god Amen. The vast temples of Karnak and Luxor stood north and south of the city and can still be visited today.

Unification The time when Upper and Lower Egypt were first united as one kingdom, in about 3118 BC.

Upper Egypt The southern region of the country. Menes, a King of Upper Egypt conquered Lower Egypt and so united the two lands.

The discovery of the Rosetta stone provided the key to Egyptian hieroglyphs.

The three great Pyramids of Giza are over four thousand years old and were counted among the Seven Wonders of the World in ancient times. The largest and oldest one, the Great Pyramid of Khufu (Cheops), contains about 2,300,000 blocks of stone, each weighing about two and a half tons.

Valley of the Kings The barren area west of the Nile at Thebes, where rulers of the New Kingdom were buried in skilfully excavated tombs. Each tomb contained the King's body in its sarcophagus, surrounded by treasures for use in the next world.

Vizier Most important of all the Pharaoh's ministers. A vizier was rather like a modern prime minister.

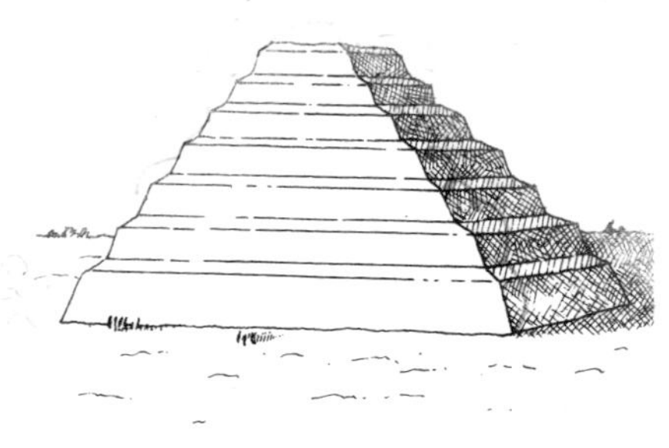

Step Pyramid

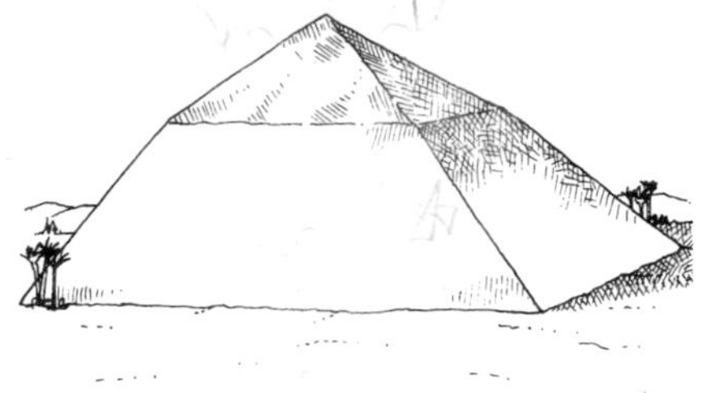

Bent Pyramid

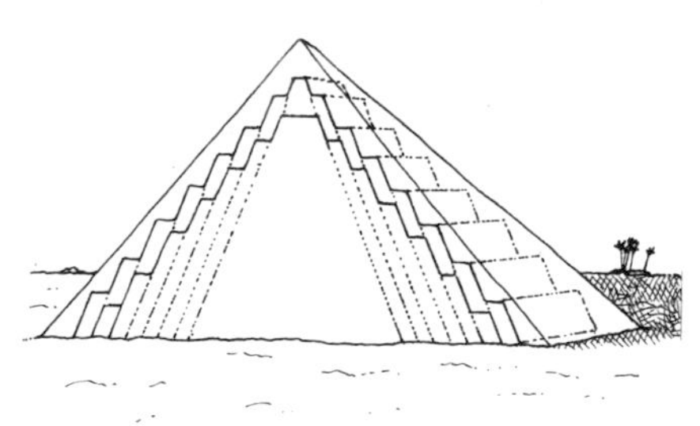

True Pyramid

DEVELOPMENT OF PYRAMIDS

These diagrams show the development of pyramids, beginning with the first Step Pyramid, built for King Zoser of the III Dynasty, by his architect, Imhotep, whose 'steps' resemble the early bench-shaped tombs called mastabas. Transition from four steps to six to eight was followed by filling in the steps with local stone and casing the whole of the outside with limestone slabs.

An interesting stage on the way to the true pyramids of Giza is the Bent Pyramid at Dahshur, for the lower part is steeper than the upper, thus producing its 'bent' look.

The great age of pyramid-building lasted about 400 years from the III to the VI Dynasty when these colossal structures were erected, each to house the body of one king. The small tomb-chamber inside the pyramid or beneath it was reached by a gallery tunnelled through the rock from the north face.

OTHER BOOKS TO READ

The Pyramids by J. Weeks (Cambridge University Press) 1971
Introduction to Ancient Egypt T. G. H. James (British Museum Publications) 1979
History as Evidence—Ancient Egypt by Rosalie and Antony David (Kingfisher Books) 1984
Egyptian Mummies by Barbara Adams (Shire Publications) 1984
The Egyptians by Anne Millard (Macdonald Educational) 1978
Egypt and Mesopotamia by R. J. Unstead (A. & C. Black) 1978

INDEX

PHOTOGRAPHIC ACKNOWLEDGEMENTS
The publishers wish to thank the following for supplying photographs for this book: Page 2 Michael Holford *left*, Ronald Sheridan *right*; 22 British Museum *top*, Ronald Sheridan *bottom*; 24–25 Michael Holford; 29 British Museum; 30 Zefa.

Picture research: Jackie Cookson